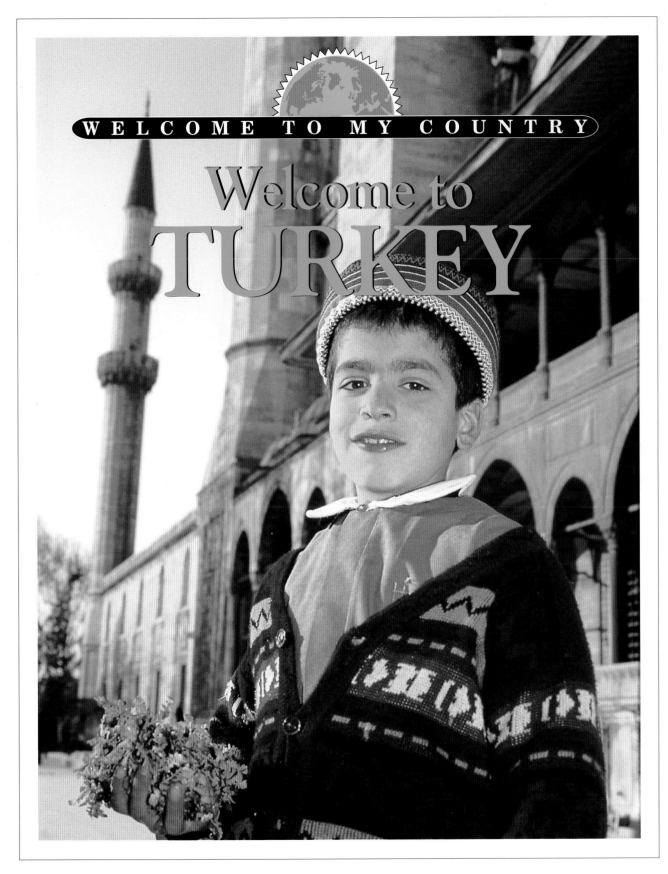

WELCOME TO MY COUNTRY

Welcome to
TURKEY

W
FRANKLIN WATTS
LONDON·SYDNEY

This edition first published in 2005 by
Franklin Watts
96 Leonard Street
London EC2A 4XD

Franklin Watts Australia
45-51 Huntley Street
Alexandria NSW 2015

This edition is published for sale only in the United Kingdom & Eire.

© Marshall Cavendish International (Asia) Pte Ltd 2005
Originated and designed by Times Editions–Marshall Cavendish
an imprint of Marshall Cavendish International (Asia) Pte Ltd
A member of the Times Publishing Group
Times Centre, 1 New Industrial Road
Singapore 536196

Written by: Vimala Alexander, Neriman Kemal & Selina Kuo
Editor: Melvin Neo
Designer: Geoslyn Lim
Picture researcher: Susan Jane Manuel

A CIP catalogue record for this book
is available from the British Library.

ISBN 0 7496 6011 2

Printed in Singapore

PICTURE CREDITS
ANA Press Agency: 22
Archive Photos: 13, 15 (bottom), 36, 37 (both)
Art Directors & TRIP Photographic Library:
    1, 7, 14, 18, 19, 20 (bottom), 24, 25, 29,
    32, 33 (bottom), 38, 40 (both), 41
Camera Press Ltd.: 15 (centre)
Haga Library, Japan: 30, 33 (top)
The Hutchison Library: 17
Images of Africa Photobank: 26
International Photobank: 2, 3 (bottom), 4,
    6, 27, 31, 45
John R. Jones: 9, 10, 23
Nazina Kowall: 3 (centre), 8, 11, 21, 35, 39
North Wind Picture Archives: 12, 15 (top)
Christine Osborne Pictures: 28
Topham Picturepoint: 16
Nik Wheeler: cover, 3 (top), 5, 20 (top), 34

Digital Scanning by Superskill Graphics Pte Ltd

Contents

Words that appear in the glossary are printed in **boldface** type the first time they occur in the text.

Welcome to Turkey!

Modern Turkey was founded in 1923. The country has a long and rich history formed by the many **civilisations** that **flourished** there, including Persians, Greeks and Romans. Lying between Europe and Asia, Turkey has a **unique** blend of Eastern and Western cultures. Let's explore Turkey and its **heritage**.

Opposite: A crowd of Turks is waiting on a **quay** in Istanbul to buy fresh fish.

Below: Kebab shops are a common sight in Istanbul and many other Turkish cities.

The Flag of Turkey

The current Turkish flag was adopted in 1936. It has a red background with a white **crescent** and a white five-pointed star. The crescent and the star are Muslim symbols. Several legends suggest reasons why they appear on the flag.

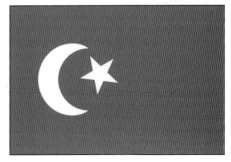

The Land

Turkey is shaped like a rectangle with an area of about 780,580 square kilometres. To the east, it is surrounded by Georgia, Armenia, Azerbaijan, Iran, Iraq and Syria. Greece and Bulgaria lie along its northwestern border. The country has coastlines on three seas, and mountain ranges run **parallel** to both its northern and southern coasts.

Below: Turkey's beautiful western coastline is on the Aegean Sea. The country also has coastlines on the Mediterranean Sea to the south and on the Black Sea to the north.

Western Turkey's coastal plains are important farming areas. Central Turkey is a high **plateau** called the Anatolian Plateau. It reaches from the northern Pontic mountain range to the southern Taurus range. Eastern Turkey has as many as eleven more mountain ranges, and they include the country's highest peak, Mount Ararat, at 5,166 metres. Turkey's largest lake, Lake Van, is also in the east.

Above: The Tigris River flows through several of Turkey's eastern provinces. The Euphrates is another major river in eastern Turkey.

Climate

Different parts of Turkey have different climates. While the coastal areas have mild winters and summers, the central plateau has more extreme temperatures. The average temperatures in the city of Istanbul, on the coast of the Sea of Marmara, range from 6° Celsius in winter to 24° C in summer. In centrally located Ankara, Turkey's capital city, temperatures range from –3° C in winter to 30° C in summer. With bitterly cold winters and hot, dry summers, eastern Turkey has the most extreme climate.

Plants and Animals

Grasslands cover much of central and eastern Turkey and the area north-west of the Sea of Marmara. Thick forests grow in most of the rest of the country. Wild animals in the forests include bears, deer, leopards and boars. Water buffalo and camels are farm animals found here.

Below:
Some hillsides in north-eastern Turkey are bare because the logging industry has cut down so many trees.

History

Ancient Turkey was called Anatolia. Signs of human life in parts of Anatolia date back to 9000 B.C., but the Hittites were the first major civilisation. They settled in Anatolia in about 1900 B.C. Not much is known about the Hittites except that they came from the north-east and ruled until about 1200 B.C. After the Hittites, a series of different kingdoms ruled Anatolia until 546 B.C.

Below: Copies of ancient drawings show us what life might have been like in Hattusas, the Hittite capital.

Anatolia was part of the Persian Empire from 546 B.C. to 334 B.C., when it fell to the Greeks. In 133 B.C., it came under Roman rule and thrived as part of the Byzantine Empire. The Seljuks, who were Turkish warriors, invaded Anatolia in A.D. 1071 and took control of its central and eastern regions. The Byzantine Empire however, did not end until Constantinople (now Istanbul) fell to the Ottoman Turks in 1453.

12

The Ottoman Empire

The Ottoman Turks first established themselves in Anatolia in the 1330s. By 1453, they had full control of the country. Their empire grew to include parts of Europe, the Middle East and Africa, but religious and economic problems during the 1500s weakened it. The empire struggled for centuries, trying to recover, until World War I (1914–1918) caused its final downfall.

Above: Mustafa Kemal (1881–1938) introduced many **reforms** in Turkey. In 1934, the Turkish parliament gave him the name "Atatürk," or "Father of Turks".

The Turkish Republic

After World War I, the **Allies** began to divide the Ottoman Empire among themselves. When the Ottoman ruler did not try to stop them, angry Turks started a **nationalist** movement led by a military hero named Mustafa Kemal. The nationalists drove out both the Allies and the Ottoman government. The Republic of Turkey was founded on 29 October 1923, with Ankara as its capital and Kemal as its president.

Opposite: This drawing illustrates the day the Ottoman Turks took control of Constantinople.

World War II and After

In World War II (1939–1945), Turkey sided with the Western **democracies**. Its own government was a democracy until the Turkish army took control in 1960. For the next twenty years, the Turkish government alternated between military and **civilian** rule. In 1983, the country returned to civilian rule and has been a democracy ever since.

Above: The Atatürk Monument in the city of Istanbul was built in honor of Mustafa Kemal, Turkey's national hero.

Süleyman the Magnificent (1494–1566)

In 1520, Süleyman I was crowned King of the Ottoman Empire. During his reign, he encouraged the growth of art and literature and introduced a system of laws. His great deeds earned him the nicknames "the Magnificent" and "the Lawgiver".

Süleyman I

Tansu Çiller (1946–)

Turkey's first female prime minister, Tansu Çiller, improved the country's economy. She was appointed in 1993, but she resigned in 1996 because of conflicts within her government.

Tansu Çiller

Ahmet Necdet Sezer (1941–)

Turkey's top judge, Ahmet Necdet Sezer, became the country's tenth president in May 2000. Sezer is the fourth civilian to serve as president. He firmly supports democracy and human rights.

Ahmet Necdet Sezer

Government and the Economy

The Turkish parliament, or Turkish Grand National Assembly (TGNA), has 550 members who are elected by Turkish citizens. Each member serves a five-year term. The members of the TGNA elect Turkey's president, who serves a seven-year term. The president appoints the prime minister, who is usually the leader of the party with the most TGNA representatives. The prime minister selects a Council of Ministers that must be approved by the president.

Left: The Turkish parliament house is located in the city of Ankara, Turkey's capital.

The Council of Ministers appoints a governor to supervise each of Turkey's eighty provinces. Each governor must be approved by the president. People in rural areas elect a village chief and a council of elders to govern them.

Between 1960 and 1980, Turkish armed forces, which include the Land Forces, Navy, Air Force, Coast Guard and armed police, took over the government three times to safeguard democracy in the country.

Above: All Turkish men between the ages of twenty and forty-nine must go through at least eighteen months of military training.

The Economy

About 40 per cent of the people in Turkey's workforce have jobs in farming. The country's main **cash crops** include cotton and grains such as wheat, rice, corn and barley. Farmers in Turkey also grow many fruits and vegetables including olives, cabbage and grapes.

Rich natural resources, especially boron, copper and chromium ore, are also important to Turkey's economy.

Above: These women remove husks from corn to earn a living.

Textiles, petroleum and iron are important export industries in Turkey, but services such as banking, tourism and telecommunications, bring in over half of the country's annual earnings.

Visitors to Turkey are attracted by the intriguing cultural mixture of East and West, as well as the historical sites, beautiful landscapes and rare religious architecture. Large Turkish cities such as Ankara and Istanbul, are particularly popular tourist destinations.

Below: Every year, millions of tourists visit Turkey's many archaeological and historical sites.

People and Lifestyle

About 80 per cent of Turkey's more than 68 million people have Turkish **ancestors** who came to Anatolia from central Asia. Another 20 per cent of the population are Kurds, Turkey's largest **minority group**. Their ancestors were **native** Anatolians. Smaller minority groups in Turkey include the Armenians, the Greeks and Arabs. Istanbul also has a large Jewish community.

Above:
Kurds look the same as Turks and belong to the same religion but they have their own language and traditions.

Left:
The ancestors of some Turks were from **nomadic** tribes such as the Seljuks.

Traditional Values

Although Atatürk's reforms introduced a modern and freer lifestyle to Turkey, many people, especially in the eastern provinces, have kept their traditional values and customs and still live by strict religious rules.

Turkish law gives men and women equal rights. Men, however, typically hold a more important position than women in society, especially within families. Even today, few women in Turkey work outside the home.

Above:
Most Turkish women still honour their Islamic faith by covering their heads when they are out in public.

Family Life

In the past, three generations of Turks lived together as a family — a married couple, their unmarried daughters, their sons, their sons' wives, their unmarried granddaughters, their grandsons, and their grandsons' wives. When a woman marries she becomes a member of her husband's family. Today most Turkish families include only a married couple and their unmarried children, but every member works in some way to help support the family.

Above: Today, large traditional families are more common in eastern Turkey than in other parts of the country.

A Turkish wedding used to be very elaborate, with a religious ceremony and a feast that involved months of preparation. Since Turkey became a republic, these kinds of weddings are held only in rural areas.

The birth of a baby has always been a time for celebration in Turkey. A new mother receives gold jewellery and the baby is showered with expensive gifts.

Left:
Modern weddings in Turkish cities are usually simple civil ceremonies.

Education

From pre-school through to secondary school, education is free in Turkey. Some children between the ages of four and six attend pre-school although it is not required. Most Turkish children start school at the age of seven. They must complete five years of primary school and three years of middle school. In rural areas, where middle schools are scarce, children are required to attend only primary school.

Below:
Turkey has about 46,000 primary schools for children between the ages of seven and eleven.

After middle school, students may choose to attend either secondary school or vocational school. Secondary schools, called *lycées*, offer a three-year course of study to prepare for college. Vocational schools offer four years of job-related training in fields such as business, agriculture and nursing. University education is limited. Only students with very high scores on a national entrance exam are accepted.

Above:
The University of Istanbul is one of Turkey's four major universities.

Religion

Islam is Turkey's main religion. More
than 99 per cent of the population are
Muslims. Following the five pillars
of Islam, Muslims worship one God,
called Allah. They pray to Allah five
times a day, give **alms**, and **fast** during
the holy month of *Ramazan*, known
as *Ramadan* in other Islamic countries.
Every Muslim is also expected to make
the *hajj*, a holy **pilgrimage** to Mecca,
at least once.

The law in Turkey allows religious freedom but forbids involving religion in politics. Public preaching is against the law, yet the government pays for the upkeep of mosques and provides religious education in public schools. Although many Turkish Muslims do not strictly follow Islamic law, most keep the Islamic holy day on Friday and celebrate the religious holidays Seker Bayram and Kurban Bayram.

Below: The Blue Mosque in Istanbul is named after the special blue tiles that were used to build its interior.

Language

Turkey's main language is Turkish which is spoken by 90 per cent of the population. The Seljuks introduced this language back in the eleventh century. During Ottoman rule, Arabic elements were added and the language became known as Ottoman Turkish. Early in the 1900s, Atatürk replaced the Arabic alphabet with the Roman alphabet. Other languages include Armenian, Arabic, Kurdish and Greek.

Left: *Milliyet* is one of Istanbul's two major newspapers.

Literature

Much of Turkey's early literature was about religion, while modern Turkish authors write about the country and its problems. Famous Turkish authors include Yasar Kemal (1923–) and Orhan Pamuk (1952–). Kemal's 1955 book *Ince Memed* is published today in more than thirty countries. Pamuk's award-winning books are published in thirteen different languages.

Above:
Bookstores are popular in Turkey, where storytelling has long been part of the culture.

Arts

Music

Turkish music reflects the country's history and ranges from traditional classical and military forms to lively belly-dancing music. The classical music of Turkey uses notes that create a "flat" sound. The military music is very loud. Ottoman bands used drums, clarinets and cymbals to drown out the sounds of battle. Belly dancing is performed at weddings and parties as well as in many restaurants.

Crafts

An amazing variety of handicrafts can be found in Turkey's famous **bazaars**. The small shops at these bazaars sell handmade lace, embroidered fabrics, baskets, pottery and even donkey's milk! "Evil eye" charms are especially popular items. Made of blue-and-white glass or ceramic, they are believed to protect their owners from harm.

Opposite: The *kemençe* is a traditional Turkish instrument. It looks like a fiddle and is played with a bow.

Below: Colourful handmade slippers are among the craft items for sale at Turkey's bazaars.

31

Shadow-Puppet Theatre

Shadow-puppet plays are an important art form of Turkey's folk culture. The plays' two main characters are named Karagöz and Hacivat. One popular legend claims that they were created in memory of two fourteenth-century laborers. An angry Turkish ruler killed the labourers when their mischievous pranks kept his building from being completed on time. Shadow-puppet performances use jokes and humour to make statements about social issues.

Left:
During a shadow-puppet performance, a light is placed in front of the small, colourful puppets to cast large shadows onto the curtains behind them.

Architecture

Most Turkish architecture is based on the simple but elegant designs of buildings constructed during the Ottoman Empire. Mimar Koca Sinan (1489–1588) was the greatest Ottoman architect. Sinan designed more than 260 buildings and influenced almost every Turkish architect after him. The Mosque of Süleyman in Istanbul is one of his most famous designs. It is the largest mosque built by the Ottomans and has schools, a hospital, stables, shops and even a cemetery inside it.

Above: The Mosque of Süleyman is a stunning example of Mimar Koca Sinan's architectural talent.

Above: Detailed Ottoman tilework decorates the inside of Topkapi Palace which was built in the mid-1400s.

Leisure

Whether dancing, enjoying a meal or just visiting, Turks like to spend time with their families and friends. They especially like getting together with people at coffeehouses. Turkey has coffeehouses everywhere. They were even there in Ottoman times when coffee was nicknamed "the milk of chess players and thinkers". Today, Turks still meet over a cup of coffee or tea to talk about world events, play backgammon or exchange stories.

Below:
Good storytellers can always find an audience in Turkish coffeehouses.

34

Turkish Coffee and Tea

Although Turkish coffee, or *kahve*, is famous all over the world, Turks actually prefer to drink tea, or *cay*. They drink it in small tulip-shaped glasses, without sugar or milk. The tea is kept hot all day without ever letting it boil so it never becomes bitter. The taste of kahve ranges from fairly bitter to very sweet. Sugar is added while the coffee is brewing to achieve the desired level of sweetness. Turkish coffee is thick and is served in tiny cups.

Above: Coffee was probably brought to Turkey in about 1555 so coffeehouses have long been a part of Turkish life.

Sports

Football is Turkey's most popular sport. The country has hundreds of teams, with games being played every week. Turkey's national teams also play in international competitions. Galatasaray Spor Kulübü, the most famous Turkish team, won the 1999/2000 Union des Associations Européennes de Football (UEFA) Cup against Britain's Arsenal.

Below: Enthusiastic Turkish football fans fill the stadiums for almost every match in the country's larger cities.

Wrestling, Turkey's second most popular sport, has a long history in the country. In fact, some of today's wrestling techniques such as the turk, sarma, eyerk and künde, were developed by Turkish wrestlers of the past. Yasar Erkan won Turkey's first Olympic gold medal in wrestling at the 1936 games in Berlin. Turkey now has about 4,000 wrestlers. Adali Halil, Celal Atik and Salih Bora are famous world champions.

National Holidays

A special day in Turkey is 23 April. It is National Sovereignty Day, a major national holiday honouring the day in 1920 when the country's government changed from an Islamic state to a parliamentary democracy. The day is also Children's Day, recognising the importance of children to the nation's future. Two other national holidays in Turkey are Victory Day on 30 August and Republic Day on 29 October.

Above:
Some children put on traditional Turkish clothing to celebrate National Sovereignty Day and Children's Day, which both fall on 23 April.

Festivals

Every year in April, May and June, the Istanbul Foundation for Culture and Arts hosts three separate festivals to promote local and international artists in film, theatre and music.

Each January, Turkey has a camel wrestling festival in Selçuk. In this unusual event, colourfully decorated camels wrestle each other until one of them falls down or runs away.

Below: At a camel wrestling festival, the camels' mouths are tied closed so the animals cannot bite each other during the event.

Food

Turkish cooking commonly includes meat, especially lamb. A popular meal called *meze* has a variety of grilled meats and vegetables. They are served with *humus*, a chickpea dip, and *haloumi*, which is grilled goat cheese.

Breakfast is usually fresh bread, spread with jam, honey or butter or eaten with salty black olives, tomatoes, cucumbers and cheese. Lunch is the largest meal, while dinner is light.

Above: Many meals in Turkey end with a sweet dessert. Fresh fruits, pastries and puddings are particularly popular.

Left: The meat for *döner* kebabs is roasted slowly on an upright skewer. Thin slices are shaved off as the meat cooks.

Kepaps, or kebabs, came from the
nomadic Seljuk Turks who roasted
their meat over open fires. Shish kebabs
are cubes of meat and vegetables that
are grilled on skewers. Döner kebabs
are made by roasting thick layers of
lamb on a large vertical skewer, then
cutting off thin slices to eat with bread
and yoghurt or humus.

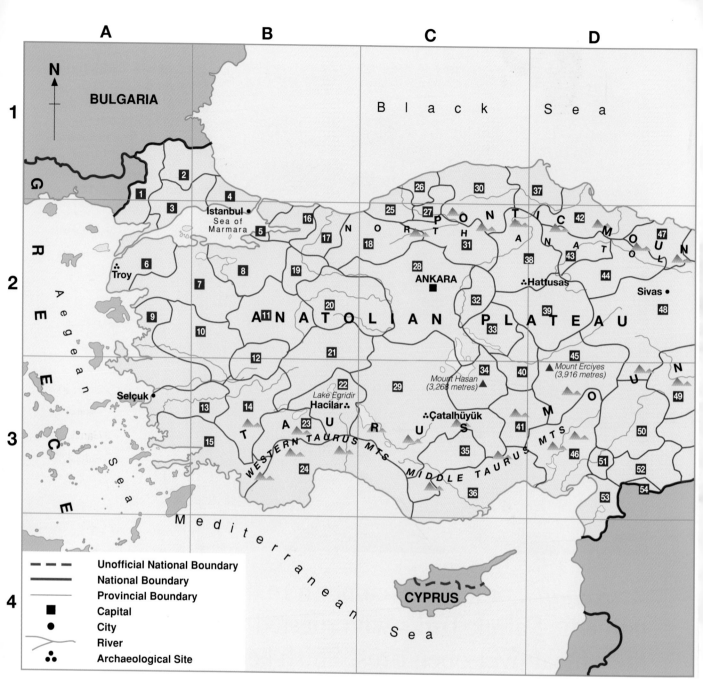

E   F

RUSSIA

GEORGIA

ARMENIA

64   65   72

55   56

73

57   58   66

• Erzurum

Mount Ararat (5,166 metres) ▲

74

59

75

AZERBAIJAN

60   67   68

IRAN

Lake Van

61

76   77

69   70

62

78

79   80

63

71

Tigris

Euphrates

IRAQ

SYRIA

TURKEY

PROVINCES

1 Edirne	**27** Karabuk	**54** Kilis
2 Kirklareli	**28** Ankara	**55** Giresun
3 Tekirdag	**29** Konya	**56** Trabzon
4 Istanbul	**30** Kastamonu	**57** Gumushane
5 Yalova	**31** Çankiri	**58** Bayburt
6 Çanakkale	**32** Kirikkale	**59** Erzincan
7 Balikesir	**33** Kirsehir	**60** Tunceli
8 Bursa	**34** Aksaray	**61** Elazig
9 Izmir	**35** Karaman	**62** Adiyaman
10 Manisa	**36** Içel	**63** Sanli Urfa
11 Kutahya	**37** Sinop	**64** Rize
12 Usak	**38** Çorum	**65** Artvin
13 Aydin	**39** Yozgat	**66** Erzurum
14 Denizli	**40** Nevsehir	**67** Bingol
15 Mugla	**41** Nigde	**68** Mus
16 Kocaeli	**42** Samsun	**69** Diyarbakir
17 Sakarya	**43** Amasya	**70** Batman
18 Bolu	**44** Tokat	**71** Mardin
19 Bilecik	**45** Kayseri	**72** Ardahan
20 Eskisehir	**46** Adana	**73** Kars
21 Afyon	**47** Ordu	**74** Igdir
22 Isparta	**48** Sivas	**75** Agri
23 Burdur	**49** Malatya	**76** Bitlis
24 Antalya	**50** Kahraman Maras	**77** Van
25 Zonguldak	**51** Osmaniye	**78** Siirt
26 Bartin	**52** Gazi Antep	**79** Sirnak
	53 Hatay	**80** Hakkari

Pontic Mountains C2–E2

Russia E1–F1

Sea of Marmara A2–B2
Selçuk A3
Sivas D2
Syria D3–E4

Taurus Mountains B3–F3
Tigris (river) E3–F4
Troy A2

Western Taurus Mountains B3–C3

Quick Facts

Official Name	Republic of Turkey
Capital	Ankara
Official Language	Turkish
Population	68,893,918 (July 2004 estimate)
Land Area	780,580 square kilometres
Highest Point	Mount Ararat (5,166 metres)
Important Rivers	Euphrates (1,249 kilometres) Tigris (525 kilometres)
Largest Lake	Lake Van (3,761 square kilometres)
Mountain Ranges	Pontic Mountains (north) Taurus Mountains (south)
Major Religion	Islam
Important Holidays	National Sovereignty Day (23 April) Children's Day (23 April) Victory Day (30 August) Republic Day (29 October)
Currency	Turkish Lira (2,667,041 TL = £1 as of July 2004)

Opposite: Handmade dolls in Turkish costumes are popular souvenirs.

Glossary

Allies: the nations that fought together against Germany and the other Central Powers in World War I.

alms: charitable gifts of clothing, food, money or other items to help the poor.

ancestors: the members of families who lived in earlier times; past generations.

bazaars: marketplaces that sell local items in small shops or open stalls that are usually lined up along a street.

cash crops: grains, fruits, vegetables and other agricultural products that are grown in large amounts to be sold.

civilian: relating to people who are not part of a police force or the military.

civilisations: societies that have highly developed cultures and governments and documented histories.

crescent: a thin, curved moon shape.

democracies: governments that are ruled by the people through their elected representatives.

fast: go without any food or some kinds of foods, often for religious reasons.

flourished: grew to be strong and healthy or successful.

heritage: anything that is passed down from ancestors to later generations.

minority group: a small cultural or social group of people who have the same race, religion, political beliefs, physical features or other characteristic, which are different from most other people in the larger society to which they belong.

nationalist: devoted and loyal to one nation over any other.

native: belonging to a certain place by being born there.

nomadic: relating to groups of people who have no permanent home and move together from place to place.

parallel: lying in the same direction as something else, but at a certain distance away that is approximately the same at any point.

pilgrimage: a journey to a holy place to show religious devotion.

plateau: a large area of flat land that is high above sea level.

quay: a concrete or stone wharf, or dock, where ships and boats are loaded and unloaded.

reforms: changes that correct faults or make improvements.

unique: one of a kind; different, with nothing else like it.

More Books to Read

Islam. Religion in Focus series. Geoff Teece (Franklin Watts)

Islam. World Religions series. Richard Tames (Franklin Watts)

Kurds. Threatened Cultures series. John King (Hodder Wayland)

The Ottoman Empire: 1450-1700. Access to History series. Andrina Stiles
   (Hodder Arnold H&S)

Ramadan and Id. Celebrations series. Mandy Ross (Heinemann Library)

Suleiman the Magnificent and the Story of Istanbul. Treasures from the East series.
   Julia Marshall (Hood Hood Books)

Web Sites

turktour.com/turkey.html

www.smm.org/catal/

www.turkey.org/artculture/

www.turkishodyssey.com

Due to the dynamic nature of the Internet, some web sites stay current longer than others. To find additional web sites, use a reliable search engine with one or more of the following keywords to help you locate information about Turkey. Keywords: *Anatolia, Ankara, Atatürk, Constantinople, Istanbul, Kurds, Ottoman Empire, Turkish.*

Note to parents and teachers
Every effort has been made by the Publishers to ensure that these web sites are suitable for children, that they are of the highest educational value, and that they contain no inappropriate or offensive material. However, because of the nature of the Internet, it is impossible to guarantee that the contents of these sites will not be altered. We strongly advise that Internet access is supervised by a responsible adult.

Index